Can I Spill My Guts For a Minute?

A R

BookLeaf Publishing

India | USA | UK

Presentation by *BookLeaf Publishing*

Web: www.bookleafpub.com

E-mail: info@bookleafpub.com

ISBN: 9789357446662

First edition 2022

DEDICATION

This book is dedicated to the person who inspires me every day. Thank you for being my muse.

#1

I would do anything
To do nothing
Next to you
Speak without speaking
The way that we do

#2

I wish I knew
When I wished
On that shooting star
Sometimes those damn
Wishes come true

I will hold you again
Either in this life
Or the next...
Until then,
All my wishes
Are wishes for you

#3

I have burned
All the books
That I wrote about you
But your name
Always appears on my pages

#4

Please don't dim yourself

You are the little boy
Singing and dancing

You are the man
With the strongest hands
And the softest touch

You will always be
The sunlight in my eyes
And the rain on my skin

#5

Drawn to the light
Of your spirit
Saddened by the reality
Of this world
Bring your magic
Back into my body
And peace to my mind

#6

I'd go to the edge of the earth
Just to watch you walk away
Drown in all the words
I never could say
Met with my dreams of you
Dreams I know
Will never come true

#7

Take me where you go
When you're lost
I will show you where
My heart flows into art

#8

I look to the sky for answers
Like the dreamer I am
The stars hold my past
The sun, my future
And the moon is my now

#9

There's a bit of you
In everything I create
You give me peace
When my world is chaos
Even when I can't see you
You're in the words I write
And the colors I paint

#10

I can still feel you
When you are miles away
Still smell you long after you're gone
I wish you'd either
Love me or
Break my heart
But you linger...
In my soul
And in my art

#11

My high
When I want to be sober
My seventeen
When I want to be older
My thoughts
When I want to feel
My dreams
When I need you to be real

#12

We can't skip chapters
In our story
If we did
The book would not make sense

Every heartbreak
Every fear
Brings us closer
Year after year

#13

We all have
A different reality
I wish you were mine

#14

Every time you break
I'm here in the darkness
Waiting for you
I try to bring comfort
As if it's the only thing
I'm on earth to do
I can't help it
That's the only thing
That feels true

#15

Can I spill my guts
For a minute?
You don't have to respond
You don't even have to read
I just need that rush
Of hitting send
Face flushed
When I see your name
Like my heart is
Jumping out of my chest
When the phone rings
That high I only get from you
When your smell
Lingers on my hands...

You're the only man
I've ever wanted

#16

How many times
Are we going to do this
Back and Forth
Neverending dance
You open up
And then close me out
You show me your soul
And then disappear

#17

Blinded by perfection
With a big smile and open arms
I will wait for you
As a lover
Or as a friend
You are the beginning
And I am the end

#18

My dreams feel like memories
And memories feel like dreams
You are always here
In front of me
Like that's how it's meant to be

#19

I hope she sees your magic
I hope she knows the universe
Is in your eyes
Because if she ever forgets
I will be happy to remind you

#20

All the years that have slipped by
And I still haven't lost hope
I'm not in denial
I know where I stand
And I'm not budging
One day
You may decide
You're ready to be loved
The way you deserve
I will be here waiting
Or I'll see you
on the other side